My Stroke of Inspiration

Paul Wokes

Published by New Generation Publishing in 2021

Copyright © Paul Wokes 2021

First Edition

The author asserts the moral right under the Copyright, Designs and Patents Act 1988 to be identified as the author of this work.

All Rights reserved. No part of this publication may be reproduced, stored in a retrieval system or transmitted, in any form or by any means without the prior consent of the author, nor be otherwise circulated in any form of binding or cover other than that which it is published and without a similar condition being imposed on the subsequent purchaser.

ISBN: 978-1-80369-998-1

www.newgeneration-publishing.com
New Generation Publishing

Chapter One

Down Kirkby Lane in the Woodhall Spa Cemetery, my friend Vic is buried. He and I were very close and, before he passed away, he promised that if I ever needed inspiration I should come and visit him at the cemetery. It is a sacred place for me. My grandparents, Vic, me one day, perhaps, lying there among oak trees, flowers people bring, fields, hedgerows, and the woods of my childhood not far from the stream my siblings and I frequented all the time on those hot and not so hot English summer days.

Across the road stands a tall oak tree where I once spent an entire night fasting and meditating.

I wrote this poem on one of my trips to the cemetery.

The Stream
I walked along the stream of my youth,
Expectant like earth in spring,
Looking for eternal life,
A way to satisfy my soul.
I found the pond fed by the stream,
Where moorhens used to nest.

Now, no sign of any birds,
Just quiet skies,
No lapwings circling overhead,
No skylarks soaring into space
Just raucous crows returning home.
Nearby I chanced upon the cemetery
Refuge from my busy world,
Where I felt life thriving, even singing.
My ancestors were buried there,
All around I felt their spirits,
Found the peace my soul craved.
I knew that I was home.

The true story in these pages was inspired by my friend, Vic, in particular, but also by other relatives and friends in the spirit world. We are never alone. Sometimes, through automatic writing, people from the spirit world dictate what we should write. With this story, I was subtly guided how best to express what was happening to me.

Vic informed me that, for the most part, he would guide me through synchronicity. Only when I had finished writing my story would he reveal the significance of my recent past, the present and the future.

In Charles Dickins' book, *Christmas Carol*, Scrooge was shown a series of dramatic events to come, ones that definitely didn't appeal to the grumpy old man. I am fortunate enough to have friend Vic to hold my hand and guide me, rather than ghosts of the like Dickins' character faced.

Chapter Two

Recent past.

16th November 2020, 16.00 hours. I am lying on my back on bed, resting comfortably, my hands on my chest. I whisper to myself: "Let the white, golden light surround my body and protect me." Then the area around my forehead starts to glow with an incredibly bright light and I leave my body through the Head Chakra. The Watcher awakens.

Twenty minutes later, Helen's voice (in my head) beckons me, "Paul, time to wake up." Immediately I am wide awake. I go into the kitchen to make myself a cup of tea. My intuition tells me to watch the next episode of *The Crown*. I am not sure why, but I follow this course of action. The episode I watch is one where Prince Charles proposes to Diana Spencer.

Synchronicity and intuition, play such a large part in my life these days, particularly after Vic told me to let synchronicity guide me, so, I knew there was a particular reason for me to watch this episode. I don't need to try and work out what the synchronicity is revealing, because it will become clear in due course of time.

For now, I need to return to the day when this all began.

☞

On Thursday, March 22, 2018, there I was in New Horizons, an amusement arcade located in the Market Place in Boston, Lincolnshire where I live. I was playing the fruit machines and winning a reasonable amount of money. I suppose I was quite happy as I had been experimenting with the manifestation of money and, being rather successful, I was pleased, though not overly excited. Suddenly, without any warning of feeling ill, I started to topple off the stool that I sat on and fell hard onto the floor. One moment I watched the reels spin, the next I fell. I was bemused by this because I couldn't stop myself from falling even though I felt as though I should be able to control my actions. I was conscious and had my eyes open throughout everything that was happening, but I was powerless to control it. I had left my body.

As I crashed down, my head cracked onto the carpeted floor. I remember several attendants rushing over and speaking to me. I wanted to reply and say I was all right, but no words came out of my mouth. One lady put a jacket under my head. I remember that, but I can remember little else. Someone must have rung for an ambulance and someone also must have rung my friend Allan Marshall, who worked locally. I knew nothing of this. Strange, though it seems to me now, I do remember being lifted onto a stretcher and carried into the ambulance. And I remember that it took an eternity for the ambulance to move off to head towards the Pilgrim Hospital. Later, Allan told me that one of the ambulance crew carried out some procedure before they moved off and this took about twenty minutes. From my recent research into post-stroke medical interventions, I understand that this likely saved my life, but certainly saved me from permanent, crippling changes to my brain and body.

Until several weeks later, I had no idea that Allan had travelled to the hospital with me, holding my hand. He didn't think I would recover from the ordeal. In one version of my life, this is where it would have ended. What a dramatic, heart-wrenching moment for Allan, and my family and friends when they learned of my death.

At that moment in time, my life was in limbo. I wasn't sure if I wanted to survive. On the one hand, I was made aware of the struggles I would have to endure if I wanted to survive and return to full health. On the other hand, my affection for and friendship with Helen urged me to fight to stay alive, to face the coming battles, challenging though they would be.

When I arrived at the Pilgrim Hospital, I remember being taken on a lift, up to, as it turned out, the ninth floor, the Stroke Unit, where I was wheeled into an office. I remember watching a large clock on the wall moving so slowly as I waited for something, anything, to change. Time stood still. I felt uneasy, restless. I didn't try to move my head because somehow, I knew I couldn't do it. Eventually, I was moved out of this office and into a ward where they lifted me onto a bed. Thinking about this now, I can't remember anyone taking my clothes off, but I suppose the nurses must have done this because, when I became a little more aware of my surroundings, I woke up in bed wearing hospital pyjamas.

I remained in limbo for the next ten days semi-consciously weighing up my options. Did I want to survive, or should I allow myself to pass to the next realm. Was this my time to die?

During these ten days I was neither fully in my body, nor totally out of it. I was having an out of the body experience. I think J K Rowling's death scene when Harry Potter goes into the spirit world, is quite accurate. I felt I had the option to join the spirit world or return to the physical world. The only difference with me was that I had more time than Harry to make my decision.

Each night, in particular, this decision became a real struggle. Getting to sleep during my entire time in hospital was a major battle. The reader might think this was because I slept in a ward with three strangers. Not so. My mother once said she could peg me on to a washing line and I would be able to fall asleep. So, why was falling asleep so difficult for me? I'm not sure. Subconsciously, I think I knew this was a crucial time. Did I want to remain in the physical world and start on the long road to recovery, or get the hell out of there into the spirit realm where I would meet Vic, my parents and so many other dear ones? During sleep this intensive battle played itself out, which is why I dreaded going to sleep. The time of my decision was getting very close.

By day ten, I had reached my decision.

Chapter Three

Dr. John, my bridge partner, visited on the first Sunday of my stay in the hospital, four days after I had been admitted. I couldn't speak, not even one word. This led to the first of many very frustrating experiences. John asked me if I would like him to contact Sylvia, one of my two sisters living in Canada, to tell her about my stroke. I wanted my family to know what had happened to me but I knew that on Monday Sylvia was being admitted into hospital herself for a serious operation. The last thing I wanted to happen was for her to postpone her operation to rush over to the UK to see me.

How could I convey this information to John? Sign language would have proved useful, but using nods and shakes of the head proved very limiting. John asked if I could write so went off to get pen and paper. I tried, but it was hopeless. My right hand was completely numb and the fingers on my left hand were no better. Eventually, John understood that I did not want him to contact Sylvia, but he had no idea why. As it turned out he wrongly assumed that I did not want my family to know that I had suffered a stroke.

Looking back now at these vexing times, the one thing I am grateful for was that my memory seemed to be working as normal. Thank goodness for small mercies.

The second and greatest frustration of my hospital stay was that I was unable to communicate with Helen, my Ukrainian friend. In 2018, I owned an ancient mobile phone with no access to the Internet, no camera or easy texting, and a battery life short enough to frustrate an angel. Moreover, it had such small keys that in trying to reply to Helen's text, I accidentally deleted her number. I now had no way of getting in touch with her. I spent many hours desperately trying to think of how I might solve this problem. I came up with no solution. This was a major frustration to me.

Not being blessed with having a wife or family, for much of my adult life I have used my spare time to coach local students in badminton, in chess, and bridge, things they would have been unlikely to come across or enjoy in those days, in the middle of a humble rural community in the north east of England. Later on, being a teacher, and understanding the benefits of a solid education, I took to sponsoring a small number of students, less fortunate than myself, but who might with help be able to explore beyond the circumstances into which they were born. One from Romania, I sponsored through to university. She graduated, later became engaged to a Swiss man and now enjoys a wonderful life free from the poverty that plagued post-communist countries. Helen, a more recent sponsored student from the Ukraine, with my help completed her degree and her masters and, but for Covid, would be enjoying a life in Paris as a consultant in the travel industry. Over the many years since I first helped her, we became dear friends, akin to close relatives, grandfather or uncle perhaps. I visited Ukraine, met some of her friends, and she has visited England. We talk a couple of times a week and help one another with whatever is troubling in our lives.

Without a doubt, I knew Helen would be alarmed to not hear from me and, owing to my age, might well assume that something bad had befallen me. Not for the first time, I underestimated Helen's determination and ingenuity. When I did not answer any of her messages, she must have guessed that something was seriously wrong and so after much soul searching chose to email Sylvia to ask her if she knew what had happened to me? Sylvia rang Dr John. And, as they say, the rest is history.

After a week or so, my speech gradually started to return, albeit mumbley and slow. At one two o'clock visiting time, I was delighted to see the Headmaster of the Boston High School walk into the room carrying an enormous basket of fruit. Thank goodness, I was now able to say a few words and thank him for this very generous gift.

Many other visitors came to see me: badminton players, bridge payers and, most surprising of all, my brother Gareth. More on that later.

Hospital life is mostly monotonous. Mealtimes and visitors, for the most part essential in keeping one's spirits up, provide a break from the dull routine.

Chapter Four

I wanted to live!

The choice was difficult and at time a close-run thing. By day ten I began to realize how difficult getting back to anything like my former state of health was going to be. True, two weeks back I might have been able to be a coach of badminton classes, but now I felt decidedly old and decrepit. I couldn't even walk or go to the toilet on my own. I am not a person who feels sorry for himself, but I was beginning to know how difficult the struggle back to fitness was going to be and there were times when I felt daunted by the prospect. I wondered if I had made the right choice.

But whenever doubts entered my mind, motivation drove me on, gave me determination to see my friend Helen again, to know how she was and if she knew what had happened to me. I feared she might think I was ignoring her. Could she think I no longer wanted to be her friend? Such fears circled endlessly in my mind while the agony of the stoke itself imposed frustrating limitations on my weak human body.

So, who is Helen and why was she such a motivating force in my life at this time and even more so today?

☙

Helen was born in Zaporizhzhia, a town of about 600,000 people. We became known to one another when she was a student studying English and German translation at Kharkov university. Sometime later, when she invited me to Ukraine, I immediately agreed to go, being excited about the prospect of meeting her. I only had one moment of doubt when I asked myself what I would do if Helen didn't turn up at the airport? My intuition told me that she was reliable and trustworthy, so what was there to fear? I had seen and spoken with Helen a few times on Skype, but I would not say enough time had lapsed for me to say that I really knew everything about her. Add to that fact, only two years before my planned visit, in 2016, Russia had invaded the Crimean Peninsula. The backdrop of my first visit to Ukraine was set against great unrest and a potential war.

I learned later that at this very juncture in the Ukraine crisis, the EU Parliament's President, Martin Schulz, described war in the country as "A genuine possibility," saying that "Something has changed" and that "Some people think that war and the risk of war is no longer a topic for discussion. If we look at events, we are talking about the risk of armed conflict."

Not being aware of this at that time, I forged ahead with my travel plans. When I told my two sisters, Sylvia and Delphine, of my plans to visit Ukraine, they both asked me if it was a safe country, particularly in light of the recent Russian hostilities in Crimea. I did ask myself how it might play out, so I had some doubts. When Helen reassured me that Kharkov was a safe town to visit, I decided to take my chance.

Just this year in 2021, I was talking to Sylvia about my previous decision to visit Ukraine in 2016. She and her husband, Ivan, told me how very worried they had been back then, being better informed on current world affairs than I was. They were amazed by my naivety! They referred to this journey as entering the lion's den! Sylvia was clearly correct in her assessment of my naivety since I had done no research but relied on Helen's reassurance that it was safe.

A documentary on Ukraine's struggle for freedom can be seen on Netflix. *Winter on Fire* describes the riots and bloody attempts to re-establish democratic freedom.

When Skyping with Helen a few weeks ago, I asked her if she thought I would have visited Ukraine if I had done my research before making a decision? She said she thought I would still have visited and she would have been right. In my defence, I had a contingency plan. If Helen didn't turn up, I would make my way by taxi to the hotel she had booked for me and then decide what to do next. Not the best of emergency plans. I was leaving a lot to chance. Or fate.

But Helen was at the airport. We immediately became good friends. Her sense of humour, reliability and kindness became easy to like. We had a marvellous time. All too short. I was sad to return to the UK.

※

Back to my time in the hospital. When, on day ten, I decided I wanted to overcome the stroke, I was desperate to renew my communication with Helen, always assuming she had not decided I was too unreliable to be her friend.

Chapter Five

The day before the stroke, I had undergone an MRI scan at Grantham Hospital. My memory remains fuzzy about this scan though I recall being put inside a drum for about an hour with headphones and microphone to allow me to communicate with the technicians carrying out the scan. At times it was incredibly noisy. However, the volume of noise didn't bother me compared to what happened immediately after my stroke.

While I was recovering in hospital, right after my stroke and for several days after that, excessive noise confused me beyond measure because I had lost the ability to isolate different sounds. If more than one person spoke, I couldn't understand anything anyone said. I guess some people say they have the same problem even if they haven't suffered a stroke. To try and explain the symptoms a little more clearly, any excessive noise jarred my entire being. I had become totally sensitive to any loud noises.

By day ten, when most of my senses were slowly returning to normal, I started to ask myself questions about the stroke. Why had it occurred? Would it happen again? Why did the MRI scan not spot the symptoms?

Writing this over two and a half years later, I am a little wiser and have some understanding of the answers to these questions. In sharing what I have learnt, I hope to make the lives of all those who have had strokes easier and give them encouragement in their battles ahead. But a word of warning. No solution cures all ills. Every person is different and that is what makes our planet so fascinating. It may sound rather morbid, but we cannot shirk the truth. After a stroke, some people make a complete recovery; others suffer further strokes and some may die.

What I do believe is that we have more control over what happens to us than we might think. I know for a fact that without a motivating reason to recover, I could easily have chosen to die.

Motivation, determination and patience are qualities we need in order to recover. And a sense to humour, though not essential, also helps.

Every stroke-sufferer I spoke to says frustration is the strongest emotion that they had to deal with. I've shared my own areas of frustration, but a new experience for me was acute embarrassment. I could go to the toilet and evacuate my bowels, but, because of the paralysis, I couldn't clean my bottom. Having to allow nurses to perform this unpleasant duty was embarrassing and demeaning. The nurses repeatedly told me that this was part of their duty and they didn't mind helping me, but that didn't make it any easier. My admiration for the doctors and nurses who work in these stroke wards is huge.

Let's lighten the mood.

About 4.00 p.m., early in the third week of my stay, the matron came into our ward to ask if one of us would volunteer to go into a different ward for a couple of nights. She said she would give us a little time to decide, but if no one volunteered she would select someone herself.

Although there were four of us in the ward, the man next to me was paralysed, unable to speak, and so needed to be in the ward because of his special care. None of us remaining three wanted to go. We'd become friends and a camaraderie had developed between us. We shared our stories, our newspapers and magazines, our food, and helped each other in any way we could. Harry (not his real name) offered to be the volunteer and we thanked him for his generosity.

Fred (not his real name) arrived at 6:00 p.m. in time for supper. Seeming to be perfectly fit and able, he walked into our ward unaided, sat next to his bed and ate his supper. *Has he had a stroke?* I wondered. If so, it must have been a mild one. After his meal, he got up and went to sit at the nurses table just outside our ward. He stayed there until 10:00 p.m., bedtime. A nurse asked him to come into our ward. For a while he sat in the chair next to his bed, but as soon as the nurse left, he shot out of the ward and headed down the corridor to the stairs. He was caught trying to leave. Back in our ward, the matron was summoned. By now the occupants of most wards were wide awake. The senior nurse tried to persuade Fred to get into his bed, but he kept asking why he couldn't go home? Stroke or not, his mind was clear enough for him to know what he wanted. He wanted to go home.

After ten minutes, the matron finally persuaded Fred to get into his bed. Well, partially. He lay on his bed, fully dressed, but telling the matron he agreed to try to sleep. The minute she was gone, Fred was off his bed, charging down the corridor. This episode was repeated many times before I finally laughed myself to sleep. One of my better night's sleep.

The next morning on the doctor's rounds, I overheard Dr. Markova talking to the junior doctors about Fred who she concluded was not suffering from a stroke, but mild dementia. When his wife came in during visiting time, this proved correct. The poor lady was desperate to get some peace and quiet and wanted her husband to spend time in a safe environment so she could get a break from his constant need for attention.

Chapter Six

Whatever country we choose to be born in—I use the word choose deliberately because I believe we have some choice in this matter—I must say that the doctors and nurses in England are fantastic. As I explained earlier, some of their tasks are not easy. Despite this, most are positive, obliging, helpful and friendly. Bearing in mind that a lot of their experiences involve coping with death, it must be hard to remain positive, particularly where death is a frequent occurrence. With the Coronavirus pandemic, which started early in 2020, more deaths than usual have been occurring throughout the World's hospitals.

Back in the 90's my father was staying with me when he had a stroke. Like me, he was admitted into the Pilgrim Hospital. Also like me, he was paralysed and could not speak, though this never changed for him and he remained semi-conscious throughout. As I explained earlier, I was uneasy at night, especially when it was time to go to sleep. During the day I was mostly calm. My father was uneasy and uncomfortable all of the time. Whenever I visited, he was constantly moving around, trying to get out of bed. Now I think of it, maybe he was trying to leave his body, or perhaps trying to go home, like Fred.

One visit, I noticed that he had a black eye. The doctor apologised, explaining that Dad had fallen out of bed hitting his face on the bedside as he fell. As a result, they fitted high sides to his bed. This made Dad even more restless as he kept trying to scale the sides of his bed to escape. Where to, I wondered?

Looking back, I wish I had the knowledge and wisdom that I have now. I would have tried to communicate with him through the spiritual world. Would I have succeeded in reaching my father, being able to calm him down and explain what was happening? Possibly. As I write this passage, I feel my father's presence guiding what I am writing. I feel very close to him, and this is a good feeling. Helen will understand the the synchronicity of this as she and I spoke about her trying to communicate with her grandfather who was suffering from dementia. Unfortunately, he died before she had the chance.

Just before my father had his stroke, I was speaking to him about passing to the other side. Dad, affectionately known as Sam, was having difficulty breathing and I broached the subject of death, not an easy one to talk about. I asked him if he thought his time of passing might be soon? He told me that he didn't think so, and we left it at that.

After his stroke, each day I went to see him, I saw different doctors. Most of them were very factual and told me the reality of the situation: my father was dying and it was only a matter of time before he passed to the other realm. But one doctor was very different. He was always positive.

"Mr Wokes, your father is a lot better today."

I guess this Indian doctor's personality was more upbeat. Who was correct? In one way, all of them were correct. Life or death are opposite sides of the same coin. Yin and Yang. Positive and negative. My father was dying, and, on some days, he was better than on others.

He never recovered his speech or his consciousness and passed away five days after being admitted to hospital.

◌⃫

This a good point to speak about the power of the individual. What powers do we have? Can we control when we die? Can we control whether we recover from a stroke or not? In my humble opinion, if we are interested in these questions, we must seek the answers from within. I am definitely interested and I am happy to share what I have found out. If my conclusions resonate with you, then they are probably true for you also.

Let me deal with the second question first. Can we control whether we recover from a stroke, or not? Yes, I believe we can, but we need motivation and determination. Do we have the power to deny ourselves a partial or full recovery, yes, I believe we do?

Now, let me consider the first question. Can we control when we die? Possibly. I am very interested in the answer to this question and am putting a lot of effort into finding out. I believe I might achieve in-depth understanding on this topic in the next few months. I am currently working on the ability to leave and enter my body at will and under control. And here synchronicity has played a part. Karan, a young man whom I coached in badminton many years ago, is now training to become a doctor. He sent me some tapes by Steve T. Jones. These tapes are about how to astral travel. They are proving very useful. Once I master this ability, I will also share my experiences with Karan.

I will now get a little technical about *neuroplasticity*. Put simply in layman's terms, this means *rewiring the brain*. The brain, it turns out, is constantly rewiring itself. If certain thoughts and behaviours are repeated often enough, a strong connection, also known as a neural pathway, is created. If you think of your brain as a dynamo, running a power grid with billions of roads and pathways lighting up every time you think, feel or do something, then this gives you some idea of how your brain works. To continue with this metaphor, some of these roads are well travelled. These are your habits, your established ways of thinking, feeling and doing. Every time you think in a certain way, practice a particular task, or feel a specific emotion, you strengthen this road and it becomes easier for your brain to travel this pathway.

I remember some wise person, once telling me not to dwell on negative thought or they could become etched into my brain. So, to give an example of this, imagine a friend has let you down badly and you are annoyed. You decide to confront your friend and he apologises. If you can accept this apology and move on with your life, then great. This is the wisest course of action and the incident will not form a regular pathway. However, if you dwell on this wrongdoing, you can see how this will affect your brain and the consequences will not be pleasant, ranging from a long-standing feud, to revenge, and, for some people, harming the other physically, even violently.

After the stroke, my brain had to create new roads, or recreate the former ones that had been deleted. In reality, this meant that I had to learn how to walk and talk all over again. To make a full recovery, I knew this would take an enormous amount of willpower, determination and effort. I chose to let my friend, Helen, became a motivating force. Anyone who wants to recover from a stroke or illness, needs a motivating force.

Chapter Seven

Gareth, my younger brother, came to visit me during my second week after the stroke. At first, I didn't recognize him. This could have been because of the stroke, but also because I hadn't seen him for several years during which we hadn't even communicated. When he walked towards my bed, I was unsure who he was, or why he was there. Once he started to speak, my memory flooded back and I realized it was Gareth.

Of course, I was delighted to see him. Of all those who came to visit me, Gareth was the most significant. Once my neural pathway lit up, I understood the significance of his visit. He had travelled hundreds of miles, all the way from the Isle of Wight, to see me. Gareth and I had always been close as children and young adults, and the long separation in communications couldn't lessen the joy that his visit brought me. Referring to the previous chapter, although my brother and I had not been close during this separation, I didn't feel hostility towards him or his wife. Sometimes life takes us on different paths and if we can accept this change without rancour or pointing a finger of blame, then we are open to a renewed friendship when the opportunity arises.

Unfortunately, Gareth planned to travel back on the same day that he visited me, so his visit was brief.

I was lucky, during my three weeks stay to have many welcome visitors. They helped break the monotony of life in a stroke ward. Only one visitor caused me stress and I had to ask him to leave. This sounds dramatic and you might imagine that this individual was a terrible person. Not so. As I explained earlier, the stroke made me very sensitive to loud noises, but it also made me less tolerant to self-centred individuals. Graham (not his real name) suffers from Asperger's Syndrome and demands a lot of attention. I hadn't recovered sufficiently from the stroke to be able to cope with Graham, hence I asked him to leave.

Once I decided I wanted to get well, I put every effort into my recovery. By day five, I was regaining my power of speech, slowly and hesitantly at first, but improving a little each day. Once the physiotherapist told me that I could go to their small gymnasium to practise walking, I couldn't wait for her to arrive each day to escort me. For the first few times, I had to be wheeled down in a wheelchair. Looking back, I still find the whole experience unbelievable. I ask myself; how could I be coaching Badminton one evening and then only two weeks later not be even able to walk? This was the reality.

The lady physiotherapist originally came from Bulgaria. I already mentioned a stroke doctor from Malta and another from Bulgaria. Now here was a physio also from Bulgaria. I hope with the EU changes that all these professionals will be allowed to stay in England. Our hospitals will struggle without their expertise.

When I arrived in the gymnasium, my wheelchair was parked close to the two parallel bars on the left-hand side of the room. The physio showed me what she wanted me to do and I was willing and keen to give anything a try. Firstly, I moved along the bars, standing between them and holding both of them. Soon I graduated to holding only one of the bars, moving along between them then turning around when I came to the end. This sounds easy enough, but believe me it was not. Turning around was the most difficult part. My legs inevitably twisted together. My right leg was so slow to respond to the commands my brain gave it. Clearly, more neural pathways needed rebuilding.

After twenty minutes the physio told me that my allotted time was over and I needed to return to my ward to rest. Sure enough, I was feeling tired, but I said I felt fighting fit and wanted to practice a little longer, if she would be so kind.

Each day of my physio session, I became a little stronger and my walking skills improved. Soon, I no longer needed to be taken to the gymnasium in the wheelchair. I could walk along the corridor at a reasonable pace.

I can still hear the voice of the physio from Bulgaria saying, "Paul, slow down."

I was in a hurry to recover. I had set myself a target of being discharged within three weeks. I desperately wanted to speak with Helen again and find out what had happened to her. I was totally motivated. I often think back to my time there and wonder what happens to those without a friend or loved one. To those whose close acquaintances have already died. How hard it must be to motivate oneself when the only expectant joy a person has is to get home to their own space, their TV, their own quiet bed. Nothing like a spell of struggling to awaken the awareness of others' much bigger suffering.

I live in a second floor flat accessed by a flight of outside concrete steps. The nurses wanted to make certain before I was discharged that I could climb up and down the steps. With this in mind, the physio took me to the stairs which run up and down all nine floors. Most of the time, people use the lifts which leaves the stairs pretty deserted. I didn't think I would have a problem stair-climbing but this proved to be another mistake. By the time they took me to the stairs to practice, I had had many sessions in the gymnasium and I was used to moving between the parallel bars at speed and turning round quite swiftly. Walking up and down the stairs sounded straight forward. I discovered that climbing stairs involved a new complex set of neural commands that I definitely had to regenerate.

I almost forgot the final, charming part of my training. A lady I had not seen before on the stoke ward asked me if I would like to practice some kitchen skills? I think she had been told that I lived on my own. Whether she knew of my single status or not, this was such a thoughtful touch that looking back I am amazed by everything they did to prepare me for discharge.

On my way to the gymnasium, I had passed the kitchen many times, but was unaware of its existence. It is a small narrow room equipped with kettle, cups and saucers, coffee, teabags, plates and a loaf of bread. The nurse asked if I preferred coffee or tea and if I would like to make myself a piece of toast? I chose tea and set about filling the kettle with water and putting a slice of bread into the toaster. Because I am always making myself and visitors cups of coffee or tea, I guess this automatically came back into my mind as my neural pathways hadn't been deleted.

When I wrote my notes about the stroke, I forgot that this training took place and never wrote about it. Now I can only surmise that I had forgotten the entire episode because so many of my neural pathways needed rebuilding that the ones that had remained intact were not at the forefront of my mind.

I want to finish this chapter by complimenting the doctors, nurses, physios and chefs. But also, all those who plan the programmes for recovery of patients both whilst in hospital and their care after discharge. In the United Kingdom this is blessedly free.

Chapter Eight

As the third week drew to a close, an unusual incident occurred. I remain mystified by what happened and the reason for it?

On Friday, almost three weeks since the day that I was admitted, at around 8:00 p.m., the phone on the nurses' desk rang. Being on speaker I could hear the caller. As this was a frequent occurrence, I didn't take much notice until I recognized the caller's voice. Ken, my nephew living and working in Atlanta, USA. Suddenly, I was alert and my mind went into overdrive. Why was Ken ringing the hospital? After the call ended, I waited to see if the nurse would come to my bedside to tell me about the call. When she didn't, I waited five minutes then rang the bell. When a nurse came, I asked her to check if Ken had called? She said there were no calls.

Of course, when you read about this, you might think that I had been mistaken. I had had a stroke, after all, and, fair to say, I was mistaken about many things, but I was certain that this wasn't one of them. I went to bed thinking to myself, *what on earth is going on?*

☙

The next day, sometime in the afternoon, Ken texted me to ask if I had received the information about his visit. Now I knew I wasn't deluded about him calling. He planned to arrive at the Pilgrim Hospital the very next day to take me back to my flat where he would stay for two weeks or so to help look after me. I couldn't wait for his arrival. The occupants of the ward noticed my excitement when I told them and congratulated me on the wonderful news. Even paralysed Harry gave me a nod.

I didn't know if the doctors would discharge me, so I summoned a nurse and asked if she could speak to one of the doctors to check.

Sometime after supper, Dr. Mangion came in to see me. He told me that I needed a few more days of rest and recuperation before I was ready to face the rigours of the outside world. He told me he understood the urgency because of my nephew's arrival, so reluctantly agreed to get my discharge papers ready.

Sunday morning and the day dawned bright and fair. Ward Nine is the highest in the hospital building and when I stood alongside my bed, I had a fantastic view of the area around Boston.

Anyone who has been in hospital in England will know that the procedure that takes the most time is getting all the necessary medication organised. The pharmacy seems to work independently from the nurses and doctors, so if the doctors order a particular prescription for a patient, it can take forever for this to be available.

I expected that Ken would be allowed to meet me in Ward Nine. So, I was very surprised when one of the nurses told me that this would not be so and that they actually had a discharge room where this meeting would take place.

As Ken travelled along the A1 towards Boston, he texted me his progress. The closer he got, the more excited I became. Of course, I was trying to contain all this excitement. I didn't want to bring on another stroke.

Ken rang me to say that he had arrived and was approaching the reception desk. I collected all my medication, clothes, papers, phone and other bits and pieces and sat in the wheelchair waiting for the nurse to take me to the lifts. I said my goodbyes and was wheeled out of the ward. The Pilgrim is a massive hospital with many corridors and rooms and the room I was led to was somewhere on the ground floor, but I had never seen it before. It was quite a large room and had a number of beds in it. I sat in my wheelchair and waited.

I had expected that Ken would be waiting there but there was no sign of him. I found this a little mysterious. Okay, it was Sunday and there were less nurses about. My phone rang again and Ken told me that he had been directed to a room which was locked. He couldn't find anyone to let him through. I told him that I was in the discharge room and he should ask whoever he saw to take him there.

Finally, five minutes later Ken appeared accompanied by Delphine, my sister, Ken's mother, all the way from Western Canada. They had colluded together to come to take care of me for a few weeks. What an amazing surprise. We had so much to talk about that we could have chatted for a very long time, but Delphine, always the practical one, said, "Okay, let's go and find somewhere to eat."

So, on Sunday, March 15, Ken pushed my wheelchair out of the main entrance to the car park where his rented car was parked. He helped me into the front passenger seat, while Delphine returned the wheelchair.

Before we went for something to eat, Delphine suggested that we should go back to my flat and have a cup of tea. I liked this idea and knew that the first thing I would do was to turn on my computer and send an email to Helen.

Ken asked me if I could remember the way back to my flat. I certainly could.

Climbing the steps outside my flat took longer than climbing the steps in the Pilgrim Hospital. They were further apart.

Chapter Nine

Motivation, determination and patience. These are the main three qualities that I believe we need in order to make a full recovery from any illness, including mental affliction. I will devote the next few chapters to exploring these qualities in relation to my stroke.

Motivation:

The first thing I planned to do when I arrived back in my flat was turn on my computer and contact Helen. After slowly and carefully climbing the eight steps outside my flat, followed by the six steps inside my flat, I planned to go into my bedroom to my computer. Fourteen steps are no climb at all when I am in full health. But the stroke meant I was nowhere near fully fit. Ken and Delphine patiently watched and encouraged my painfully slow step-by-step climb. Finally reaching the landing of my flat, I changed my plan, headed for the front room and collapsed onto my sofa.

After Delphine had made us all a cup of tea, we chatted about our immediate plans: sleeping arrangements, going out for something to eat, shopping, and other details. They both had questions about the stroke. When did it happen? What had happened? Was I conscious during the stroke?

Over two years have passed since the stroke and I now am a lot clearer on such matters. Back then, I had to try and work them out. I particularly struggled with the question about my state of consciousness. Only recently, I had the presence of mind to go back into the New Horizons Amusement Arcade to ask the staff if they remembered such details. All three of the attendants who dealt with the emergency remembered that I had my eyes open throughout my ordeal. Interesting, because as best I think my state of awareness could've been summed up as *the lights were on, but nobody was home.*

Before we went out to eat, I told Delphine and Ken that I needed to turn on my computer to see if I had any urgent emails that needed answering. Once on my email site, I saw that there were hundreds of unread emails. I had no time to check them all, so I just pressed the compose button and typed in Helen's name and it came up with her email address. Thank goodness for automation and thank goodness my memory had not been totally wiped out. I typed her a very short email telling her that I was back home in my flat and would give her more news later on in the evening. I felt so relieved.

Why is motivation such an important quality after a stroke? Let me start by explaining how the physicality of the stroke affected me. After the stroke, my energy levels were always extremely low, each new physical endeavour being a personal battle to be overcome. After the excitement of my release from hospital, Ken and Delphine stood by me every step of the way, tying my shoes, helping type emails as I had become fumble-fingered, cooking my meals, cleaning the flat.

However, when they returned to their respective homes in USA and Canada, imprisoned in my flat, unable to drive, struggling with the simplest of tasks, motivation to recover, to return to some functional degree of my past life drove me daily. Without that motivation and its partner, determination, I could have slid into despair, I could have become a crippled, useless old man dependent on others for the simplest of joys.

No. Everything in me refused to accept that my past life had ended, but instead I determined to overcome the mental block of walking to the store, the irritation of not being able to click the mouse, and motivation became the catalyst that made that happen. Others played a part too.

Physiotherapists employed by the National Health Department came round to visit me every day. This was tremendously helpful as they oversaw my recovery and gave me a list of daily exercises to follow. When asked, they answered questions about when I would be able to drive again, how quickly my hand and finger co-ordination would improve, how far I should try to walk.

This after-care support was so vital that I would have struggled without it. One of the caregivers asked me if I had thought of applying for a disabled persons' Blue Badge for my car once I could drive again. She offered to help me but even so the form took me quite a while to fill in and answer all the questions about how far I could walk and how much recovery time I needed. I hadn't actually done much walking since the stroke, so some of the answers were guesses.

I have struggled with asthma since I was a child, having had two previous close calls with death, one time collapsing unconscious for hours in the middle of a lonely road in the middle of the night. The years of asthma attacks also weakened my lungs and heart which put me face-to-face with my maker one other time when I became so weak that I couldn't walk across the room. This wouldn't be the first time a Blue Badge could have come in handy. Some weeks later, one arrived in the mail.

One time, after I had finished doing my exercises, I was relaxing in the front room with my caregiver when she asked me about my physical goals. I told her that I would like to walk to downtown Oldrids, so I could have a meal there. I expected her to encourage me with this goal, but she startled me with an emphatic, "Good gracious, no."

I looked at her quizzically, waiting for further explanation.

"That is much too far for you to walk at present."

This store and restaurant are about two miles from my flat, so I was surprised at this lady's reasoning.

A few days later I reduced my goal to walking across and down the road a few hundred feet to the local garage for a Mr Sub takeaway. I made it there with several stops to rest along the way. What should have taken me no more than five minutes took an epic forty-five minutes. Two and a half hours later, back home, I was completely exhausted. Slowly, but surely, I began to see the enormity of the recovery task ahead of me. Without my driving desire to re-join my bridge matches, to plan trips to visit my nephew and sisters in North America, and to see my friend Helen, I would not have succeeded.

From the outset, I knew Helen wasn't just one more of my students that I wished to help. I felt a connection and hoped very much to get to know her better. Explaining why events happen and their significance after the event is easy. Doing this beforehand, not so easy.

On my first visit to Ukraine, Helen and I visited the Gorky Amusement Park in Kharkov and spent an enjoyable afternoon walking around the park taking photos and taking a ride similar to the London Eye before travelling back on the trolley buses to the Paris Restaurant for a meal. When Helen told me that we needed to cross the busy main road to catch the next trolley bus, I hesitated and suggested that maybe we should stay on the same side of the road. But Helen was in touch with her friend, Alina, by phone, and assured me that we needed to go to the other side of the road. Once on the trolley bus, I was watching the direction of our travel and we seemed to be going further and further away from the city centre. Helen finally agreed with my assessment when we stepped off the bus in the middle of nowhere. She told me that she could call for a taxi, but had no way of knowing where we were. I suggested we walk to the nearest junction to find a street name.

Haven't we all been in that kind of situation many times. Lost, confused, perhaps exhausted, frustrated. No easy solution. It is in times like these that that a person's character is exposed. Are they liable to blow their cool and blame someone else or adapt, cooperate, and act patiently? Helen is the latter.

Fast-forward to when Helen visited me in Boston and we planned a trip to Sandringham Estate to visit the Palace and Grounds. That Sunday the extensive car parks overflowed with visitors' vehicles. Desperate people had parked anywhere. I parked under a cypress tree on one of the many ways in.

I had never visited Sandringham before so, as a teacher, I found the palace particularly fascinating, allowing me to imagine a past filled with Royal intrigues and historic moments. The extensive gardens with their magnificent trees and flowers capped off the lovely day. When it was time for us to leave, after searching endlessly up and down rows of cars, we still hadn't found my car. Helen suggested that I sit on a park bench while she tried on her own. Half an hour later Helen returned to my bench. Still no car.

She flopped down next to me. "Okay, what we do next?"

"Where did you look?" I said.

She pointed out her huge path through the car-parks maze.

"Then it has to be in this other direction, right?" I said. "Let's try together."

Five minutes later we found the car. Wearily we both climbed aboard planning to stop for a meal on the way back. Helen was quiet for a while and then she started to chuckle.

"Do you remember the time in Kharkov, when we got lost on the way back from Gorky Park?"

We both began to laugh.

Chapter Ten

Determination

The Oxford Dictionary describes the word determination as a firmness of purpose. Without a huge amount of determination, it would be impossible to overcome the effects of a major stroke.

Once I had decided I wanted to recover, the fact that I was relatively fit for my age (asthma and my heart troubles notwithstanding), and bore little excess weight, helped enormously as I learned how to walk and climb again. Rewiring of the neural pathways gradually followed. When it came to learning how to speak again, I found it important to keep my brain active, forcing myself to remember past situations, people's names, math formulae I learned in Grammar School, the dates of British Kings and Queens, famous battles, and more. When I couldn't remember, I would think for days knowing that the memory was in there somewhere, wracking my brain, circling the point in time, sometimes conceding and looking it up.

Before dementia starts or after someone suffers a stroke, I recommend keeping the brain active by playing bridge or chess, doing crosswords, solving sudoku puzzles, even reading a few Pulitzer Prize winning books. Every mental activity, however little, helps. "If you don't use it, you lose it," applies to brains as well as muscles.

Of course, there are many qualities that came into play during my long road of recovery, but *patience* stands out as a key quality.

Chapter Eleven

Patience

I am not a very patient person. My older sister, Sylvia, would be the first to tell me. Without patience, frustration creeps in. I am not going to make excuses. I know I need to work on this. After my stroke, this weakness became significantly more apparent.

I became *so* impatient.

In my mind's eye, I could see exactly what I wanted to do and how it could be done, so I resented the fact that physically I could not immediately achieve the objective.

When using the techniques of manifestation of a desire or idea, I've learned that first we use thought about what we wish to create followed by raising this idea to what some see as the head chakra from whence we can send it forth into the universe. However, from thought about the idea to its manifestation can be a long delay. I admit I get impatient by this.

After the stroke, many months passed before full dexterity returned to my right hand. Being right-handed, this posed endless battles: my fingers struggled to hit the right keys; my thumbs and fingers refused to text correctly on the ridiculously teeny keyboards on my mobile phone. More than once I hurled my computer mouse at the wall. Apologies to all mouse lovers.

If you have troubles with being patient, don't give up. With a determined effort your former abilities can slowly return. The writing of this is proof, because I am typing it on my computer, with my taped-together mouse. ☺

During my post-hospital recovery, walking was extremely slow and tiring. Even now I can only walk slowly, but I do feel less tired than I used to.

One day I came up with the great idea of riding my bike. So, I wasn't allowed to drive. Fine. I would ride down to Oldrids for a meal. I hadn't used my cycle for several months prior to the stroke. But, being the eternal optimist, I thought I would could just hop on and pedal off. After all, one of my exercises, set by the physio, was to sit on a large rubber ball, take my feet off the ground and then pass objects, of different sizes, to the physio. At first, I did wobble a little, but soon mastered it. Biking, I concluded, would be a doddle.

The bike tires turned out to be as flat as doormats and I couldn't find the correct valve to pump them up. Where had I hidden this valve? I kicked the bottom drawer closed. I banged my cupboard door. Grr.

The following morning, having slept on the problem and remembered in the night where I kept valves (getting the mind to bring things up in sleep can be very effective), I returned to the garage. Pumping up the bike tires took a monumental physical effort followed by a coffee break rest-and-reward before I once again stood there, house locked, ready to go. Oldrids, here we come.

Lifting my right leg over the seat, I knew would be a challenge, but I had a plan. I would use my concrete steps, instead, giving me the necessary elevation. I was ready to launch. Feet on the pedals, I pushed off, wobbled, and toppled straight over. Bruised, I got up, stood back on the steps and tried again, and again, and again.

Over and over, I tried, each time with the same result. Every damn time, I wobbled and fell over. Somehow, in addition to limited muscle movement, I had lost my ability to balance. I am not a quitter, but I knew that this was a mental, more than a physical problem. I pushed the bike back into the garage, put the lock back on and turned the key.

Back inside the flat, I made myself another cup of tea, sat down on my sofa and planned what to do next. A little meditation brought inspiration. I remembered that not long ago I had been teaching a friend's young son, Harvey, how to ride his new bike. The very lad who named my car the Red Rocket. I remembered telling him to keep upright in the saddle and to not move his body right or left when turning. I realized that I must have been doing just that instead of staying still. The following day I decided to try again.

I did succeed, not immediately, but eventually. Finally, I had found a degree of freedom that prior to the stroke I had taken for granted. Now I could get about more quickly and go further without being as tired had I walked. Of course, the first time I tried to stop, I braked so hard that I lost control and careened into a garden fence.

This wasn't the first or last mishap along the way to recovery.

Chapter Twelve

Throughout my recovery, and the adventures this entailed, I was in communication with Helen, who at this time was living and working in Kiev. Fairly soon after the stroke, Helen suggested that I come to visit her in Kiev so she could look after me, since I have no relatives nearby in Boston and once my sister and nephew Ken had returned, apart from the care worker visits, I spent the entire time alone. This idea appealed, though I was concerned that my visit would negatively impact Helen's studies and life. She insisted it wouldn't and said that was what friends were for. All I had to do was to make sure I was fit enough to travel. My immediate reaction was less than sensible. I would book a flight *that very day* to fly out within the next few days. The more cautious side of me said, *Hold on a minute. You can't even drive yet.*

Towards the third week of my time in hospital, I asked one of the doctors when I would be able to drive again and they suggested about four to six weeks after I had been discharged. Believe me, without wanting to wish time away,

I was counting down the days to when I could resume driving my car.

As I pointed out previously, some memories returned almost straight away but others took a lot longer to surface. As I am writing this chapter on December 5, 2020 two memories have just resurfaced. When I visited New Horizons to ask about my state of consciousness during the stroke, all three of the members of staff who witnessed my stroke said that, while I was laying on my back waiting for the ambulance to arrive, I was frequently glancing at my watch, even though I couldn't speak or get up. They wondered why. I just remembered that I had parked my car in the Boston Market Place, in a one-hour parking zone, and I must have sub-consciously known that the hour was about to lapse. If I had been able to speak, I would have been like the white rabbit in *Alice in Wonderland* constantly looking at his watch and muttering, "I'm late, I'm late for a very important date."

One of my neighbours helps the local council get ready for market days. He told me later that he spotted my abandoned car, and being aware of my stroke, kindly moved it to a Council-owned parking area.

Once I had learned again how to ride my bike and dismount without crashing into garden fences, driving my car became less important. But, riding my bike to Heathrow to fly to Kiev? I don't think so! So, the plan to take a trip to

Ukraine became a new motivation to get driving again. The physiotherapist who helped me fill in the form for my Blue Badge told me that I needed to complete one final test before asking my doctor for permission to resume driving. I became all eagerness to make it happen.

She was evasive about the nature of this test which left me speculating about perhaps physically sitting behind the wheel of a car and going on a test drive. It turned out very different from anything that I had imagined.

The test was timed. I can still remember some of the questions. I was given a random letter of the alphabet chosen by the physiotherapist and then asked to write down as many words as I could think of beginning with this letter, but I was not allowed to include any proper names. Other questions included looking for the odd one out from a group of images. Another involved following a set of instructions. For this question, she produced six squares, six triangles and six circles in three different colours (blue, red and green; two of each colour). I remember she asked me if I was colour blind and then read out the instructions, slowly and carefully, but only once. She was not allowed to repeat any instruction. Put the red circle on the blue triangle. Put the blue square on the red circle. In all there were ten instructions to follow and I got nine out of the ten correct.

Another question, I was told, was designed to eliminate any confusion that might occur when driving. I thought to myself that it was probably about not getting distracted by trying to change the cassette while driving, and definitely not reading text messages while driving.

My assumption was wrong again.

The lady gave me a piece of paper with a story written on it and I was asked to underline two key words which were written many times in the story. Not too difficult, right? The only problem was that at the same time she read aloud a different story and I had to make a note of all the times she mentioned the number eleven. I certainly needed to be alert to complete this task. The reading was conducted at a steady speed and when she finished, I was confident that I had done reasonably well.

I think the attitude when taking such a test is all important. I looked at it as a challenge, but a fun challenge. I needed to pass, but if I failed, I would retake the test as soon as I could. I was buoyed by the fact that my father took his car test over five times before he finally passed. For sure, I would leverage some of this determination, one of our family's strongest traits.

The final question was the most interesting. In front of me were placed two test tubes, one containing a small ball at the bottom; a bowl full of water; a piece of rubber hose; a pair of sugar tongs; and a small rubber bung. My instructions were to remove the small ball without turning the glass tube over to tip it out.

Just a great puzzle. Right up my alley. I love puzzles. I wondered who had designed it.

Two minutes. No problem. *This will be a doddle.* The timer clicked on.

I took the empty test tube and filled it up with water from the bowl. I planned to fill the other test tube, containing the ball, with water, expecting the ball to rise to the top of the tube from where I could use the sugar tongs to pluck out the ball. I had a plan. But, as I started to fill the empty test tube with water, the water ran back into the bowl. I was confused. I scanned the other items, thinking of an alternative way to solve the problem. My intuition told me that the way I had chosen was the right way. I looked more closely. The test tube had no bottom in it. Bingo. I inserted the small rubber bung, which was an exact fit, and then proceeded with my original plan.

At the time, I wasn't sure how passing this test equated to me being ready to resume driving. I have more understanding now. Along with all the physical exercises, passing this deductive reasoning proved that I had also overcome the mental aspects of the stroke, which, if remaining, could have impaired my driving ability.

After Ken and Delphine's visit in April when I was discharged from the hospital, to my delight, Ken returned in June of the same year. By now, I was back driving my car although, to be fair, I had not covered any great mileage, only short journeys. At my suggestion, Ken did not rent a car this time. On arrival at Heathrow, he travelled by train to Peterborough where I planned to meet him. Boston to Peterborough station is approximately forty-two miles, a medium distance journey. No problem.

Later, when Ken was due to return to Heathrow to fly back to Atlanta in the US, I boldly insisted on driving him to the airport. There and back the combined distance is approximately 270 miles. Again, no problem. I managed both ways without mishaps, though I was quite weary at the end of it.

By September, I felt I was definitely fit enough to travel to Kiev, although I did have a concern about being able to walk and carry hand luggage down the long distances from check-in desks to the departure lounge, and so forth, in some airports. Thankfully I wasn't going to Vancouver, Canada, which has marathon-length corridors, or so it has seemed in the past. I consoled myself with the thought that if I allowed plenty of time for this task, I could stop and rest along the way. I suppose I could have asked at the check-in desk if they could arrange transport for me. My pride got in the way of such a sensible idea, wanting to prove to myself that I had fully recovered from the stroke. I hadn't, though I was doing very well.

Once seated in my window seat, I was so happy to be travelling to meet Helen once again, maybe even a little complacent. What I soon came to realise was that even normal activities had to be undertaken with care. When the air-stewardess reached my row, I ordered a sandwich and an orange juice. I have always loved travelling and I was sitting back, relaxing, looking forward so much to the coming holiday. I smiled, imagining strolling around the sights in Kiev, as I reached for and knocked over the damn orange juice. In trying to stop the liquid pouring from my small table onto my cream-coloured trousers, I fumbled again spilling even more of the orange liquid all over my trousers, shoes, socks and seat. What a clown! I silently cursed. I knew Helen would be sympathetic to my plight, but I wasn't trying to win her sympathy, I wanted her to see me perfectly fit and healthy.

Helen met me at Kiev airport. We were both delighted to see one another again and planned right away to get out of there. She had ordered an Uber taxi and, once outside the airport building, used her mobile phone to find the cab. On our way towards the centre of Kiev, we caught up on news and in no time the hour's journey had passed. Helen had booked me a room in the same massive apartment block that she lived in while working in Kiev. She was on the fifth floor and I was on the third floor.

Helen is an excellent timekeeper, very trustworthy and reliable. It is a quality that I value. It is therefore easy to imagine Helen's concern when I failed to be available for our previously planned Skype session, the day I had the stroke. On my holiday, if Helen said she would come to my room for 10:00 a.m., she would knock on my door at precisely 10:0 a.m. Several times, we walked to a nearby restaurant about a kilometre away. She was patient with my slow walking pace or the times I just had to rest and recoup.

Some days we would travel by taxi to a different part of town to have breakfast or lunch. After this light meal, we would walk round a church or museum. In one church, I watched a Christening service fascinated by how close we were able approach the proud parents, with no one being offended. The Greek Orthodox Christening service seemed very similar to our own Anglican Christening services.

During my stay, Helen arranged for me to have a massage by a professional masseuse, years of asthmatic breathing issues having distorted my muscles and frame; I find a deep massage can ease my tight muscles and allow me to breathe more freely.

As Helen worked during my visit, sometimes I stayed in my apartment and used Helen's laptop to write or play chess.

Helen had promised to look after me while I was in Kiev and she did just that. While I didn't need her to do anything, it is always a special treat for a bachelor to get their washing and ironing done and meals cooked. Every evening I enjoyed a delicious vegetarian meal prepared by her especially for me, since she isn't a vegetarian.

Admittedly, Delphine and her son, both good cooks in their own right, had done the same when they visited me in April, though one can never get enough of a good thing.

Although Helen had some things of her own to take care of, even when she was not physically present, I felt she was there in spirit. When she was present, she devoted her entire energy and attention to me.

I was part way through writing my novel, which I had decided to call *Court* 13, and Helen was typing out some of my ideas when I asked her if she would help develop two of the characters. Right away, she warmed to the task. I gave her the overall plot and scenario used to show these characters involvement in the drug trade. Other than this, I gave her a free reign. To be honest, Helen proved to be a better writer than I was.

I can't recall exactly how long I stayed on holiday in Kiev. I do know that the time passed in the blink of an eye. It was soon time to return to the UK. If I could have stayed longer, I would have done so. I was sad to be leaving.

In the early hours of the morning, Helen travelled with me to Kiev Airport and watched me pass through the security area before waving goodbye. She had made sandwiches for me to eat in the departure lounge, very helpful since vegetarian food is hard to come by at Kiev Airport, and Helen's sandwiches are delicious.

I munched miserably on my sandwiches as I worked on a Sudoku puzzle to pass the time. I heard no announcements that my plane was boarding but, being so wrapped up in my own misery at leaving, my mind wasn't really on the time.

Finally, I stood up, ambled over to the desk and showed them my boarding card and passport, at which point their panic set in. They rushed me down the stairway into a taxi which took me to the plane. Everyone else had boarded and they were all waiting for me to arrive. All eyes were on me as I walked down the aisle to my seat.

So ended the most wonderful holiday I had ever had.

Chapter Thirteen

The Watcher

In this chapter, I am going to examine some of the aspects of life which I would like to know more about. By allowing my thoughts to flow freely I am hoping my intuition will kick in and reveal some insights about these topics.

I have always believed in reincarnation and the immortality of the soul, probably because my siblings and I grew up in a home where our father was loosely connected with the Theosophical movement started by Helen Blavatsky in the late 1800's. I also remember a book my father owned on the near-death experience of a woman who died and visited a wonderful realm of loving beings and extraordinary beauty. Many call this Heaven, though the millions of near-death experiences now available in books and YouTube films say it isn't an exclusively religious place for any one group of followers. Rather it is the dimension to which we all will go when we leave this temporary shell called a body.

For these various reasons, I have never feared death and think that life and death are just two different states of consciousness.

I like to think of awareness as being like an observer or Watcher of our true selves, our inner being or soul. When we are in a state of total awareness, the Watcher observes what is happening, without prejudice.

In meditation, when we closely observe the rhythmic nature of our breathing and concentrate only on this, we can allow the Watcher/soul to take over. When I do this, the third eye, below my head chakra, starts to glow and throb in a positive way, not in a painful way. The more time I spend in this state of awareness, the more control I have over my physical and spiritual life.

Over thirty years ago, something happened to me which I have often wondered about, since I feel that all significant life events are for a purpose. Possibly now, having worked through the tapes of Steve T Jones, I might gain an understanding of its purpose. At the time, after it happened, being busy with life, I pretty well forgot about it. Looking back, I wish I had investigated it more fully.

I had been in Whaplode helping a friend, Joanne, with some decorating. The work created a lot of dust and I should have given more thought to this because of my asthma, dust being a trigger that can onset breathing problems. I left just before midnight to travel the fifteen miles back home to Boston. I had almost reached the outskirts of Boston when an asthma attack gripped my chest and my breathing became badly laboured. Stupidly, I had forgotten to take my inhaler with me. As I drove down West End Road, the asthma attack grew worse.

If you have ever been close to a person suffering from an asthma attack, you would become aware that their breathing had becomes strained. What you probably can't imagine is that with a serious attack the airways become so swollen that the sufferer feels they are drowning for a lack of oxygen. They bend over in an effort to take in enough oxygen to stay alive. Before I had medication to ease these terrible symptoms, an asthma attack could last for several days of a waking, living hell.

We take for granted our ability to breathe clean, oxygenated air, which is probably why cruel and wicked humans use waterboarding and other oxygen-deprivation techniques to torture poor souls into telling their secrets for a release from the torture.

Imagine then the quirk of nature that allows a baby to be born with all the problems asthma brings to its life.

Back to that time, just past midnight, in a quiet rural setting, my body wheezing away, bent over the steering wheel, I knew for a fact that as I struggled to breathe and the oxygen levels in my lungs depleted, they likewise did in my brain until it became very muddled. In this confused state, my brain was telling me that if I got outside the car there would be more oxygen for me to breathe.

On this very cold December night, I opened the car door, left the engine running, and went and laid across the front of my quite old car, which Harvey, a dear little five-year-old boy that I knew, had nicknamed the Red Rocket. I tried to take a few deep breaths, but naturally there was no more oxygen outside the car than inside and the air was so much colder that it became even more difficult for me to breathe.

Just when I was starting to despair, a car passed me going in the opposite direction. It stopped twenty metres away to allow a young lad to get out and go to his house. In a pathetically weak voice, I tried to cry out.

"Help, help, help."

Neither driver nor passenger so much as looked my way. My befuddled brain tried to ask what I could do to attract attention, all the while a dominating thought trammelled through my mind, *I'm going to die. This is it. I'm done for.*

The young lad disappeared inside the house and the car drove off.

Then, as my body began to shut down, my bowels loosed as I fouled myself, I slithered off the car to the ground. Before I lost consciousness, I remembered that I had not written any will. *Who will get my money?*

I ask myself now, did that even matter, but at the time it seemed to matter a lot.

As death approached, my breathing eased. Everything became very peaceful, without fear or pain.

I remember nothing further until 6:00 a.m. So, what state of consciousness was I in lying there on the cold road? Was I dead? Was I in a coma? Was I in a state of hibernation? I should have asked more questions of the doctors who treated me. If I were to speculate, I would say the Watcher was allowing me to decide whether to return to earth or progress to the next realm. I am convinced that a link exists between this event and my time in hospital right after the stroke. On both occasions I was deciding my next course of action.

Do we have a choice of whether to live or die? Possibly? At some point we are due to leave planet Earth and whether we have control over this moment in time remains to be seen. I will let you know as soon as I find out!

I can remember the doctor who treated me after this near-fatal asthma attack asking what he should do with my soiled tracksuit. Throw it away, I told him. He said they could have it washed. I was adamant that they should throw it away not liking the feeling of embarrassment or the idea of someone handling my stinky clothing.

Before he left, the doctor asked me if I needed anything else.

"I just want to go to sleep," I said. "I'm so, so tired."

"You mustn't do that Mr. Wokes," he said. "The oxygen levels in your lungs are much too low. We need to allow them to fill up."

Clearly, during the six hours that I lay on the roadside, I wasn't sleeping. Also, unlike an animal that wakes up after months of hibernation, hungry but well rested, I wasn't hibernating either. I was extremely tired.

At 9.00 a.m. the doctor returned to check my oxygen levels, telling me that I could now go to sleep if I wanted. In no time I fell into a deep, dreamless sleep.

Around midday, when I awoke, the nurses asked me if I wanted food or drink but I told them I just wanted to go home. The summoned doctor appeared concerned.

"Mr Wokes," he said, "You had an amazing escape. You should have died from hypothermia or as a minimum suffered severe brain damage from an acute lack of oxygen. Neither happened." He paused as his mouth pursed. "We would like you to stay in hospital for a few more days so we can complete further tests."

"I would like to return to my flat," I said.

He didn't seem too happy about that but said he had no other reason to insist that I remain in hospital, so went to prepare my discharge papers.

Not long after, still wearing a pair of hospital pyjamas, I was taken by taxi to West End Road where I had left the Red Rocket. It had been pushed off the road into a farmer's field that ran alongside the narrow, minor road. The engine was off but the keys were still in the ignition.

The taxi driver waited as I started the engine. I gave him the thumbs up and drove off back to my flat, exhausted, but none the worse for wear. Back home I made myself a hot cup of tea, grabbed a handful of biscuits and fell into my easy chair.

Looking back over this event, and my stroke some thirty years later, twice now I have skirted the border between this realm and the next. Did I have a near-death experience involving visiting the heaven state or hover above my body as doctors tried to revive me? No. However, on both occasions, I had the power to make a conscious life or death choice. What happened was miraculous. Life itself is miraculous and any incident involving life and death is worth studying.

Synchronicity. A few weeks ago, I watched a nature video in which Chris Packham spoke about animal hibernation. In the documentary, he spoke about a Canadian who collapsed on the side of the road in winter temperatures of minus twenty degrees. Before he was rescued, the man froze solid. My sister who lived for several years in Yukon, Canada, also told me of a Native woman in the 1970's who likewise became so cold that her body completely shut down. At the time, it was the coldest temperature on record that a human body had fallen and recovered. Both, miraculously, made a complete recovery. Possibly my roadside asthma attack and recovery followed similar patterns. Cryogenics au naturel.

Chapter Fourteen

Synchronicity

The Oxford Dictionary describes *synchronicity* as an event that occurs at the same time or rate. I like to think of it as events or occurrences that are linked, in time and space, to previous incidents or experiences of a similar nature. Spiritual pointers, if you like, that confirm that we are on the right spiritual track, though we don't always realize their significance. The more we operate from the third eye and head chakra, the more we notice such events and appreciate their significance. My friend, Vic, promised to guide my spiritual journey through synchronicity. While I don't spend time looking for significant events, I do believe they are occurring more frequently.

When working with Helen and Karan, I have noticed that many more synchronized events occur than when I work alone. A few months ago, Helen recommended that I might like to watch, *The Queens Gambit* on Netflix, a mini-series about a young girl who played chess really well. Before I even started to watch the series, I realized a synchronicity of this series. Back when I was a university student, I broke the world record by playing chess continuously for 68 hours.

When, my sister, Sylvia, and Helen were helping me with the editing and writing of my novel, *Court 13*, I was writing about the character Sam Witherspoon, the investigative journalist in my story, I remember thinking what a fluke it would be if one day Reese Witherspoon would read my novel and want to make a film of it. Wouldn't that be an interesting case of synchronicity at work?

A few weeks ago, I had an eye infection and decided to get help from an optician. I ended up by having a complete eye test, which I had never had before, much to the amazement of the optician. I pick up and use off-the-shelf reading glasses now and then, and they seem to work for me. The Indian ophthalmic optician asked me if I had any recent illnesses. I told him about my stroke.

"So why did you have a stroke?" he said. He repeated himself three times.

I had never thought about the question and no answer came to me. I guess I might have said that I had no idea.

Later, when I returned to collect my prescription glasses, I decided that if the same optician was in the store, I would give him the answer to his question.

"I hadn't finished my work on earth and needed more time and knowledge to help others undergoing similar experiences."

His innocent question triggered much meditation and thought and gave me an understanding of the stroke and why it had happened to me.

Chapter Fifteen

Karan, who I mentioned earlier, is training to become a doctor. As part of his training and specialization, he offered to come and visit me to chat about the stoke. His visit coincided with the Coronavirus pandemic, so we arranged to sit outside on my patio where there are outdoor chairs and a table.

Karan explained about neuroplasticity. This shed light on aspects of the stroke. His explanations helped me understand why I had to rewire so many of my neural pathways.

We also talked about samadhi, a Buddhist term meaning a state of meditative consciousness. Ever since the stroke, I have been working on my ability to leave and enter my body at will. Why? That is an important question and one that needs answering. Both the asthma attack and stroke made me curious to find out more about sleep and what happens when we go to sleep. Why is it sometimes difficult to get to sleep? Why do some talk or even walk in their sleep? What level of consciousness exists when we sleep? What are dreams and their significance? Do we all dream?

Many questions, few answers. Perhaps samadhi might provide me with answers.

When I was at Hull University, in the 60's, I developed the ability to have a short sleep during the day, using no alarms or devices, though not during lectures, tempting though that was. If I had to finish an essay, a brief nap allowed me later on to work until 2:00 or 3:00 a.m. and still wake up at 9:00 a.m. in time for breakfast and lectures. At that time, I didn't have the same time control that I do now. Today, it is a measured science.

My friend, Joanne, was fascinated by my sleep research and suggested that I take it a stage further by carrying out a few experiments while I was asleep. In one experiment she suggested was that once I was fully asleep, someone quietly approach and pinch my arm, or stick a sterilised needle into my arm to see what would happen.

œ

Some time ago, in Leeds, I was hypnotized by a medical doctor interested in regression into people's past lives. I asked him if he believed that people had lived these past lives. He had an open mind on the issue, he replied. Possibly they had led the past lives, but equally they could be inherited memories from another's past.

Having listened to and made notes on Steve Jones' tapes up to and including Modules 9, I believe astral travel—also called astral projection—is certainly possible, which is motivating me want to achieve it. I found the tapes inspiring, feeling myself in tune with what Steve Jones spoke of, though what he speaks of is not my ultimate goal. Who wouldn't want to freely and consciously astral travel to wherever we want, proving our capability by say, travelling across nations to where a friend or relative lives and being able to read something they left out for this purpose and in the waking state confirming and recording the accuracy?

Would such a thing be a useful exercise, I suppose if I was interested in solving murders, or catching evildoers in their act or treachery, but more important for me is knowledge about my body and its functioning awake, in sleep, during astral travel, or during hypnosis.

When the doctor in Leeds hypnotized me, I was sitting on a chair in his lounge. I remember him putting me into a trance. I also remember that although I had my eyes closed, I could hear everything going on, but couldn't see anything. When I listened to Steve Jones' Module 9 Tape B, he mentioned that in astral traveling, although our eyes are shut, we should be able to see all around us for three hundred and sixty degrees. I can't do this. I need to find out how to open my eyes once I am in the trance state.

During the hypnosis session, I remember the doctor's wife coming into the room and asking the doctor if he would like a cup of tea. The doctor then said to me,

"Mr. Wokes, you don't think you're hypnotised. Is that correct? So, try to open your eyes."

I tried and couldn't.

In the hypnotic trance, we are under the control of the hypnotist. I guess there's nothing wrong with that provided the hypnotist is an honourable person, though I confess I am a little wary of allowing anyone else to have control over me like that.

Some years back I took a trip to the US where I met up with my nephew, Ken, in Las Vegas. We decided to go to a show purportedly by a hypnotist. We agreed before the show that if the hypnotist asked for volunteers, we would both put up our hands. Sure enough, not far into the show the hypnotist asked for volunteers so we raised our hands. Ken was one of ten people selected. The hypnotist then conducted a simple experiment to decide which three out of the ten he would ask to take part in his show.

Ken wasn't selected, but before he left the stage, he was asked to check his weight on a set of scales, which he did. The scale recorded what Ken felt was his true weight. I believe this was repeated for the other seven rejects. All confirmed the same thing. The hypnotist then stood on the scale and several people confirmed that he weighed about 280 pounds. Not a small man.

He then put this very small, petite woman into a deep hypnotic state and told her she was going to become an iron bar with the strength of such a piece of metal. She was asked to lie on her back across two tables separated by a metre. With her feet and knees resting on one table, her chest, neck and head on the second table, the hypnotist climbed onto one of the tables then started to jump up and down on the woman's unsupported stomach.

Quite disturbing to see, but a clear demonstration of the power of hypnosis. Other equally amazing acts followed. After the show, Ken and I spent a long evening trying and failing to debunk the veracity of the evening's events.

ଔ

According to Steve Jones, it is easier to astral travel if you are in a trance. Does that make it an illusion, like bouncing on a person's stomach, though it surely looked genuine to us? So, is astral travelling a genuine reality, like this three-dimensional realm? I just watched a television programme on mathematics, including the topic of small sub-atomic particles called quarks and how they don't follow logical patterns. Maybe our astral bodies are like quarks, so they don't follow logical patterns.

I have considered asking if Karan can arrange for some sleep experiments to be carried out in a research laboratory.

If by examining my sleeping mind medical students can learn about the brain, I would be happy to co-operate.

One day when a local decorator was working on the landing outside my bedroom, I told him that I was going to have a short nap.

"Okay," he said, "I'll shut your bedroom door."

"No, thanks," I said. "Please leave it open."

He looked surprised, but moments later, before I dropped off, I imagined my body wrapped it in white and golden light, told myself to wake up in twenty minutes time. Despite having an "intruder" and noise a few feet away right outside my door, I left my body and woke up exactly twenty minutes later.

I joked about not falling asleep in university lectures, though I remember an incident that happened at Hull university. The day of my 10:00 a.m. history lecture, I woke up with an asthma attack. At that time there were no asthma inhalers to relieve the severity of an attack (and my father had cautioned me not to consider the use of adrenaline as a solution because of its health hazards, he being a third-generation pharmacist). I had two choices. I could stay in bed and skip the lecture or I could ignore the asthma and go to the lecture.

I chose the latter.

Fortunately, I owned a car, one of the few students in those days who did. Maybe this and the fact that I really enjoyed the history class, swayed my judgement. But outside the lecture room, builders were drilling. The professor did his best to make his voice heard above the drilling noise, but at the back of the hall where I sat—feeling unwell made me want to shy well away from the action—it was even more difficult to hear what the professor was saying. The hot and sunny day overheated my body. The noise and worsening asthma attack together worsened my breathing. To help my struggling mind concentrate, I gave up and laid my head on the bench in front of me. I continued to listen to every word the professor said about Henry VIII's foreign policy. The prof thought differently.

Suddenly, my friend Keith tugged my arm and I sat bolt upright. The professor stood at the front pointing his finger at me and ordering me to get out of his lecture. Being picked out like that when you're your body is screaming for rest, oxygen, and an easing of its agony, you feel little inclination to justify your need to rest your head. Over two hundred students stared as I stumbled past one row of seats after another on my way to the exit at the very front of the lecture theatre. It was the most embarrassing moment of my life.

Brooding about life's unfairness while still struggling with the asthma attack, I fell into my car and set off back to my lodgings on Anlaby Road. Driving on the dual carriageway at about 40 miles an hour (the speed limit for this stretch of road) I followed the slight right-hand bend when suddenly a cyclist appeared right in front of me. I jammed on my brakes, but had no hope of missing the cyclist. One minute he was in front of me; the next he flew over my car.

My car screeched to a stop.

I had recently watched a documentary about accidents and remembered that moving a person after an accident could be fatal. Leaving him in the middle of the dual carriageway while I went to call for an ambulance hardly seemed sensible either (no mobile phones back then, of course). He would likely get run over or killed, if he wasn't already dead.

I stumbled from the car and went to look for signs of life in the young lad lying in the road. As I approached the boy, I heard him muttering. *Thank goodness he's alive*, I thought. He appeared unconscious, but breathing, so I made a decision, picked him up and placed him in the front seat of my car. I then drove to the nearest hospital where he was taken inside. Before leaving, I gave my name and my landlady's phone number and asked them to call me with news of his progress.

Before I was able to go back for some much-needed sleep, I drove to the Police Station to report the accident. An officer took down my statement.

But I lied.

It was not a total lie. Most of what I said was true. I'm not making an excuse, as lying is inexcusable, but our egos are there to protect us in times of trouble. If I had told the exact truth, the police might have investigated further, I told myself, and I didn't want that hassle. It was unlikely that I would face serious blame for the accident, but I desperately wanted to forget everything about the whole sorry day. Of course, by telling a lie, I made certain that the incident would remain in my mind to never be forgotten. That is what happens when we lie.

Had I been my normal, observant self, would I have been able to stop before hitting him? Possibly! The brakes on my car were not very efficient, like most cars back then compared to modern cars, but the question of whether I could have stopped or not is not relevant. My problem was that I did not see him until he was right in front of me.

My next lecture was the next day at 2:00 p.m., so I asked Nancy, my landlady, to wake me up before dinner. I told her about the accident explaining that the hospital might call. A few minutes later I was soundly asleep in bed.

When I woke, Nancy told me that the hospital had rung. The lad had regained full consciousness around 3:00 p.m. and after the doctor's examination he was allowed to go home. Apart from biting his tongue as he landed on the road, he was unharmed. This turned out to be the first of three miracles that I played a part in.

☙

Some years later, as I drove my car to a remote area where I planned to give a friend a driving lesson, we watched in horror as a car raced up behind us, at double the speed limit straight for a corner. Sure enough, the eighteen-year-old failed to make the turn, his car flipped right over, then rolled three more times in the air, crossing the nearside ditch until it landed upside down in a field. My trainee driver and I jumped over the dyke and rushed into the field to help. Checking and finding that the boy appeared to have no pulse, the student said, "We have to lift his car and get him out."

"You're joking," I said, not being Arnold Schwarzenegger, but I grabbed the car's bumper and started to lift the car. To my shock, we heard the boy start breathing. The weight of the car on top of him had been blocking his airway. For fifteen minutes the student and I held up the car, our muscles screaming for relief, but we knew that if we let go, he would likely stop breathing again and die. It was a real life and death situation.

After what seemed like an eternity, another car came by and together some of the occupants helped hold up the car while others pulled the young man out from it.

In this miracle number two, had we not witnessed the accident and acted so promptly, Mark Regnier would have died. Happily, we helped to save his life. Both the student and I received a Police Commendation for our actions.

The other miracle involved me helping someone who had a crippling drug problem to get into rehab. Without my intervention, that person could also have died.

☙

With the miracle in Hull, that evening I drove around to see the lad. He wasn't home, but his mother was delighted to see me. She profusely thanked me for taking care of her son, Roger, who she described as a bit of a tearaway. A few months earlier, he had ridden his bike downhill straight into the back of a parked lorry. This made me feel slightly better, but didn't excuse my lie, which continues to haunt me, even today.

Chapter Sixteen

The Watcher and the brain.

Helen has played a key part in the writing of this memoir. Also, I sense, somehow, that stepping closer to the after-life realm, has allowed me to liaise with my friends in the spirit world. In some respects, they have inspired what I write. You could call it a form of automatic writing, although no one from the other realm has dictated what I write. Perhaps they watch over and help me choose the right words. Along with meditation, this guidance from the spirit world helps me gain an insight into the true nature of our being. I feel privileged to experience this.

On this day, Wednesday December 12, 2020, I knew what this chapter had to be about. At 9:00 a.m., I texted Helen to say I had sent her an email. Shortly afterward, she asked me to check if I had sent it. As I read her text, I knew that I had not sent her the email. I thought I had sent it, but in reality, I knew I had not.

Since the stoke, I have learned to double-check my actions. I might be heading to the Boston Market Place to take a document into my bank. When I arrive and park, I realize that I have not brought the document with me. We have all had similar experiences in the pressure of living in the 21st century, and particular those of us who have passed our seventh decade. Previous to the stroke, age notwithstanding, my mind was sharp as a razor. I seldom made such mistakes and my life was pretty well organized. The stroke had definitely messed with my brain.

A different term for the Watcher might be mindfulness or awareness. Some part of my brain knew that I had not sent the email that I wrote about above, another insisted I had sent it. The Watcher or soul monitors the brain and, if we allow it, can help in this respect. The more time we spend remaining mindful, or, as I speak of it, with the Watcher observing our lives, the more control we have over what happens. When I finished writing the email to Helen at 1:00 a.m., because it was so late, I decided to save it in my draft box rather than sending it. As my custom had been to send emails straight away, the neural pathways believed this is what I had done, so they told my brain I had sent it. This leads me to one of my favourite pastimes: bridge.

After the stroke, I was very keen to start playing bridge again. I have played bridge since the sixties when I learned it in university. In no time, it become one of my main forms of recreation and social interaction. I have played and coached children and adults in the wonderful complexities of the game and written and published a book on the subject. I have played competitively for fifty years, and reaching the level of a Life Master bridge player in Britain has been one of the great joys of my life.

My stroke had the potential of stealing this great joy from me. For weeks, as I struggled to talk, then walk, this fear lurked in the back of my mind like a letter that you refuse to open because of the bad news it might hold. What if I couldn't play bridge ever again. What would I do with my days? Stare at the TV? Mope on my couch? Not being the moping type, I told myself and anyone who asked, that of course I would play bridge again. "You watch me."

When my bridge partner, John, visited me in hospital, he brought some articles from a well-known former England bridge player about how to conduct the auction when you have an opening hand, with support for your partner's opening suit and a singleton or void. I studied these articles in great detail. It helped wile away some of the time as I recovered and helped keep my brain active. Once I was discharged, I was raring to get back to the game, while wondering how any memory loss might affect my ability.

Not long after, I headed over to the Tennis Club where the local bridge club met. Most of the members had learned of my stroke and were keen to hear news of my recovery. I was trying to give a hundred percent concentration to the bridge.

Thankfully, I had not forgotten about the bidding convention system that John and I play. However, I made a few errors, most because I relied on my intuition and didn't always doublecheck using my known logic techniques.

During coffee break, John explained how he has to check everything at least twice, or he is prone to make mistakes. John has to take a lot of medications because of an ongoing battle with cancer and the meds sometimes makes him drowsy, he explained. Interesting how our own ailments can help us sympathise with others.

Clearly, like John, I would now need to exercise the same amount of caution. The stroke had changed the way my brain worked. I needed to be slower and more careful. The Watcher and my intuition work at an incredibly fast speed, faster than the speed of light, but my poor brain was on a go-slow! What John told me made sense and I was able to make the necessary adjustments. I still use my intuition, but I now check all my plans at least twice.

In this chapter I have tried to explain the role of the Watcher and its importance in our lives. Of course, many people do not believe in any form of afterlife or a Watcher. That's okay. Those comfortable with such concepts might find it helpful.

How can we recognise this awareness, this Watcher? Each person can look for their own signs of his presence. I use the male terminology, but the Watcher or Soul is neither male nor female. It encompasses both genders. All religions and spiritual explorations struggle to explain and express the Divine.

When I place my attention on my third eye (head chakra), the Watcher appears and I feel my head glowing. Everyone can observe the Watcher at work. Imagine that you are a person who gets very angry. One day, you lose your temper with your friend. Anger is a normal human emotion, but if you feel the anger coming on and watch the anger arising, can you stop it from manifesting? Who is it that watches your actions? I call it the Watcher. If you can identify with the Watcher instead of being totally absorbed and involved in the emotions themselves, then your spiritual life will be enhanced beyond all measure.

Here's another example. You are going to confront your boss about some action that seemed unfair to you. This actually happened to me when I went to see the History lecturer who threw me out of his lecture during my asthma attack. Rather than going in determined to seek an apology, go in as an inquirer rather than an accuser. When the Watcher is present, we are so much more powerful.

Here is an example for one of my friends. When you face a challenging situation, try and observe what is happening, including the emotions that are arising. Watch and observe, rather than getting drawn into the emotion itself. If you can let the Watcher (awareness) take over, then you stay in control of the situation.

I know, easy enough to say such words, not so easy to practice them. Emotions, we are told leap into existence ten thousand times faster than thoughts, but deciding to try to step away from emotions is the beginning of mastery. I don't pretend to have mastered this by a long shot. I have failed on many occasions, most recently with a relative, but I keep on trying. If I can manage to achieve it on just one occasion, it could become easier on the next. According to St John's Gospel, when Jesus was brought before Pilate, the Roman Governor, he controlled the interrogation. The Watcher gave him the confidence to observe what was happening rather than being drawn into the emotional life and death struggle he was facing.

The more we become aware of the spiritual realm and allow ourselves to be guided by it, rather than trying to control what happens in the physical world, the more contented we become and the more control we actually have. So much of the physical world is a paradox.

Chapter Seventeen

Some of my friends and family say I have had a difficult time for much of my life. Aside from the stroke, I had a pretty serious tumble some years back when a railing broke and I fell and broke my hip in such a way that the femur was thrust up into my abdomen. On another occasion, a bout of flu turned into an infection of my pre-existing weak heart which nearly ended up killing me. And then asthma attacks my entire life have ended up giving me a bit of a hunched back as if I had been bowed over with the weight of these troubles.

But to me, I say, troubles be damned.

No doubt old age brings difficulties. I often say that old age is a bummer, but life in itself is wonderful and I believe we have a lot more control over what happens to us than we might at first think.

I chose to recover from the stroke. I was not forced or coerced in any way. At some moment in time, we have choices of life or death to make. Our lives are played out against the backdrop of this physical world. Some have uneventful lives. Others, like myself, have dramatic events taking place quite a bit of the time.

The Coronavirus has made all of our lives more challenging. No longer can anyone say their live is boring. We are involved in a life and death struggle.

Some people are lonely with few friends, if any at all. It is incumbent upon all of us to engage in our local community and befriend those who are lonely. Over my life I have made many friends. As a teacher, I interacted with thousands of pupils. All of them had their own story to tell and their own life to lead. I hope I inspired some of them to reach for their true potential. But, above all else, I hope they made many friends along their journey.

At some point in our life, we might choose to live in a monastery or self- isolate, but ultimately, we need to have friends to share our lives with. Mankind is a social animal and without company we could go mad.

I want to finish by thanking all of you, some of whom I have met and some of whom will remain anonymous. I hope you have gained benefit and enjoyment from reading about my exploits with the stroke.

I also want to thank my family and friends who have remained loyal to me throughout my life and a special thanks must go to Helen. She will always have a special place in my heart.

Acknowledgements

As the author of this book, I have received inspiration and help from both the living and those who have passed into the spirit world. Vic, who is buried at the Woodhall Spa Cemetery, was a close friend when alive and it was through his inspiration from the grave that this memoir came to be written. Olena (Helen) was the motivation behind my full recovery from the stroke and remains a close friend and custodian of my secrets. Karan helped me with the medical aspects of the stroke and encouraged me with my writing. Katy designed the book cover and liaised with New Generation on the printing and publishing. Delphine, my sister, edited the manuscript and supported me in creating my best writing.

Without help and support from these friends, relatives, and the nurses and doctors who tended me, the book wouldn't have been possible.

www.ingramcontent.com/pod-product-compliance
Ingram Content Group UK Ltd.
Pitfield, Milton Keynes, MK11 3LW, UK
UKHW041943230426
12048UKWH00008B/110